Biography

James Egan was born in in 1985 and lived in
Portarlington, Co. Laois in the Midlands of Ireland for
most of his life.
In 2008, James moved to England and studied in Oxford.
James got married in 2012 and currently lives in
Hampshire with his wife.
James had his first book, 365 Ways to Stop Sabotaging
Your Life published in 2014.
He has also written his No. 1 Best Seller, 365 Things
People Believe That Aren't True.

Books by James Egan

365 Ways to Stop Sabotaging Your Life
365 Things People Believe That Aren't True
365 More Things People Believe That Aren't True
Another 365 Things People Believe That Aren't True
500 Things People Believe That Aren't True
100 Classic Stories in 100 Pages
1000 Facts about American Presidents
Words That Need to Exist in English
The Pocketbook of Phobias
Adorable Animal Facts
1000 Inspiring Quotes
1000 Amazing Quotes
1000 Historic Quotes
Inherit the Earth
Fairytale

How to Psychologically Survive Cancer

By

James Egan

ISBN: 978-1-326-44492-1

Lulu Publishing Services rev. date: 10/10/2015

Dedicated to all of the brave people who battled against cancer

My Uncle Jimmy

My neighbors, Joe and Nora

My friend, Donovan

My Da

And My Wife, Julie

Content

__INTRODUCTION__

After my wife battled with cancer, she said she should write a cancer survival book.

But after some thought, she reconsidered because she didn't want to re-visit the worst time of her life.

A lot of people close to me have battled and even died from cancer recently; my wife, my father, both of my neighbors, my close friend and one of my best friend's mother have all had it in the last few years.

I talked to them about writing a book like this. They all thought it was a great idea but they didn't want to do it themselves for the same reason– they didn't want to relive the worst experience of their life.

So I have decided to use all of their testimonies as well as my own observations and research from the whole experience.

I saw a grief counselor, Mark, when my father was gravely ill, who assisted me with this book as well and to him, I owe my thanks.

If you or someone close to you is diagnosed with cancer, doctors and surgeons and nurses will bombard you with biological words, clinical terminology, medical mumbo-jumbo and complex details about medication, treatment, surgery, injections and so forth.

When my wife, Julie, was in hospital, sometimes a doctor would come in, talk to my wife and I for ten minutes about her results, then leave, and we wouldn't have a clue if what he said was good news or bad news. All we heard was hospital-babble. If you keep hearing words like, "carcinoma situ polycystic annular pancreatitis lymph nodes irregular estrogen levels" your brain can't process it.

All Julie wanted to know is, "Will I be okay?" And unfortunately, the doctor didn't answer that because we got lost in medical jargon.

What's worse is that this is very common.

You don't need to have a biological understanding of how treatment can make your marrow debilitate on a cellular level or how PET scan works (but that's not going to stop the doctor from telling you every single detail in a clinical manner.)

Your body is putting up a huge fight against the illness and the treatment but your mind is putting up one hell of a fight too.

Your body will be fighting this a lot of time, but your mind will be battling the cancer ALL of the time.

If you or someone close to you is diagnosed with cancer, you will want to read everything possible about treatment, wigs, headscarves, chemotherapy, radiotherapy, medication, statistics, etc.

But a lot of books and doctors won't focus on the psychological side at all. They will vaguely reference that you will feel depressed and you need to stay positive and do activities to alleviate your mood.

But everyone knows this. If you have cancer, you need something more specific than that. It's easy to say you need to feel positive but you don't know how until you have experienced cancer. You may not be aware of how much it affects your mental state.

That's the purpose of this book. No clinical terminology or scientific mumbo-jumbo. These are unhelpful to a person battling for their life.

This book is to give you an understanding of the mental state of a person combating cancer and how to deal with it.

Sometimes I will repeat some information. I don't mean to be repetitive but I have to in case you are looking at certain chapters or there is a specific chapter that you want to look at. So if you get sick of me saying the same facts or statistics over and over, I do apologize, but I need to stress every factor of the cancer process to do this book justice.

Okay, let's start with the biggest question…

<u>WHAT IS CANCER?</u>

Before I start talking about the psychological side of cancer, you will need to understand cancer itself.

It is extremely complicated how cancer works. It involves mutations in your DNA, which damage your genetic makeup on a cellular level. My wife would be scrambling through books and the Internet, trying to find a description of cancer in a simple, down-to-earth way. When you fear for your life, you don't have time for long-winded biological explanations. You want an answer that anyone can understand.

Here is mine.

Cancer is not a disease. Diseases can be contagious but you can't catch cancer from somebody else.

Cancer is simply an abnormal growth in your cells. Your body is made up of ten trillion cells. That's 10,000,000,000,000 cells that make you you. Most of your cells look like oval-shaped blobs. Imagine these cells form a flat fluid river. Most of these are wedged right beside each other like a body-sized jigsaw.

Once too many cells build up on top of each other, the rest of your cells break away from the abnormality to avoid building up too much. This growth is known as a tumor. If the cells break away from the growth successfully (which it usually does) the tumor will be harmless and is known as a benign tumor.

If the cells didn't break up in time, the growth will become so big, other passing cells will start to clump with it. Every time a cell latches onto it, it increases in size by the tiniest amount but it means it is even more likely that another passing cell will latch onto it. It works exactly like a snowball rolling down a hill; the more mass it builds, the faster it builds even more mass. This means that the growth will grow faster over time and once it starts to cause damage, it is known as a malignant tumor. The other word for this is cancer.

To understand this better, let me use an allegory. Remember that river of cells image I mentioned above? I want you to picture an actual river. This river represents your cells. Every droplet of water is one single cell.

Now let's say that over time, the waves of the water knock a large rock from the edge into the river. Let's say this rock is circular, two-foot-wide and weighs fifty pounds. This rock is so heavy that when it lands in the water, it doesn't budge. The force of the river can't force it to roll. It's stuck and there's no way it's moving anytime soon.

So what happens? Does it stop the river flow?

No.

The water will simply flow around it. It's a very minor diversion that will have little to no effect on the river.

Or so it would seem.

Over time, other objects are going to knock into the rock. Pebbles, branches, garbage. Nothing big. Nothing dangerous. Nearly every object that hits the rock will bounce off it before getting caught in the current and passing around it.

But every once in a while, something will hit that rock a specific way. A large branch could hit it and get wedged in the river. This wedge could allow the branch to collect lots of stones and twigs. Before you know it, the water will stop pouring through the rock. The water will be trickling through at a snail's pace.

Now picture this – what if a mile down from the river, there is a fishing market at an exact location where they rely on catching fish to fund their business? How are they going to catch fish now that the water has been diverted? So it's not just affecting the river or fish but people and their businesses.

In this allegory, the rock is obviously the cell abnormality. When it cuts off the water, that's the cancer cutting your organs ability to perform its function (breathe with your lungs, break down insulin with your pancreas, digest with your stomach, etc.)

The failing fish business represents the people around you who also feel the affects of cancer. Cancer doesn't just affect the person who has it. It affects everybody. It affects your family, friends, classmates, coworkers; everybody is in this together.

As soon as you are diagnosed with cancer, you will want to start treatment as soon as possible. This usually comprises of chemotherapy and radiotherapy. Let's look at chemotherapy next.

<u>WHAT IS</u>
<u>CHEMOTHERAPY?</u>

Chemotherapy is the most common treatment for cancer. Soon after you have been diagnosed, you are normally brought to hospital to begin this treatment. A nurse or doctor will hook you up to a machine through your vein where chemicals will be poured into your bloodstream. This is normally done through the arm or through a porter caffe. A porter caffe is a surgical incision in your chest where the chemicals can be inserted directly. Some people prefer this, as it can be frustrating to try and find a vein in the arm, which can make patients angry or anxious.

It can take several hours for the chemicals to enter your bloodstream. The chemotherapy session is usually completely painless.

The purpose of chemotherapy is to poison the cancerous cells. The chemicals are attracted to cells that divide rapidly (like cancer cells.) A chemotherapeutic drug that attacks rapidly dividing cells is called a cytotoxic drug. The downside to this chemical is that many of your normal cells divide rapidly as well. Since the chemicals pass through your bloodstream, the chemicals will poison most of your cells – good or bad. Hair follicles, the digestive tract and bone marrow are examples of cells that divide rapidly. This is why many chemo patients will lose their hair, have intense bone ache and suffer vomiting and nausea.

The idea behind chemotherapy is that your cancerous cells are too young to be fortified. Cancer cells are only a few weeks or months old. They should be so fragile that the poison should exterminate them.

Although it kills a lot of your healthy cells, these type of cells are several years old so they are much stronger and should be able to regenerate. In fact, many cells should grow back stronger than before, much like a broken bone becoming harder after it heals. This is why hair grows back thicker.

There are countless concoctions of chemicals that can be used for chemo but they usually fall into four categories.

Each of the four chemicals tends to have a side effect – agony, hair loss, weakened immune system and nausea. You might only get one chemical or you might get all four. Four chemicals tend to be for patients who have very little chance of survival. If you don't get the four chemicals, you shouldn't experience all of the side effects.

My wife lost her hair but she didn't experience the agony that is associated with chemotherapy because she didn't get that specific drug.

My father didn't lose his hair but he did experience agony because he was given the chemical with that specific side effect.

Your doctor will be able to tell you which drugs you will receive in your treatment so you will know what to expect before experiencing the side effects. There will never be a scenario where the doctor says you won't lose your hair and then it falls out. You won't be caught off guard like that. If you get that chemical, you lose your hair. If you don't get that chemical, you keep your hair. It's that simple.

After your first chemo session ends, you will experience the side effects soon after. The side effects can come within hours or days. The timing of the side effects is usually pretty consistent. If you felt the side effects two hours after your first session, it will probably happen for the rest of your sessions. If you experience the side effects four days after your first chemo session, that's probably how it's going to be for the remainder of your treatment.

Usually, chemo treatment is composed of six sessions every three weeks. This should give the patient enough time to heal for each session. So the whole process should be about three months.

After the three months is up, the patient normally finishes their treatment with radiotherapy.

WHAT IS RADIOTHERAPY?

Radiotherapy normally begins several weeks after chemotherapy ends.

A radiotherapy machine will fire a laser in the area that the cancer resides in. This procedure normally takes about fifteen minutes. This treatment is most common with breast cancer. The person may not experience much pain, but they will feel very tired. The tiredness is not what you experience from a lack of sleep. The fatigue is similar to jetlag or how you feel after an intense workout. It may not seem as bad as chemotherapy but it's a different type of battle.

You see, as awful as chemotherapy is, it is only made up of six sessions. Radiotherapy is normally composed of twenty-five sessions. Most patients have radiotherapy five days a week for five weeks. Patients tend to have a radiotherapy session Monday to Friday. Then they rest during the weekend. If they are still feeling tired on Monday, they still have to go for their next session. And the next one. And the next one. And they only get two days break per week for five weeks. Because of this exhaustion, some people consider this harder than chemotherapy.

The majority of people shouldn't experience pain but it does happen. If the laser was fired into the breast, that part of the body will probably be hypersensitive for some time. If the laser was fired into the stomach, this can irritate your digestive system or bladder, which can cause great discomfort and pain. Several weeks after radiotherapy, your doctor should let you know what the results are, what the next step is, how effective was the treatment, what has happened to the cancer, etc.

__ARE THERE EXCEPTIONS?__

Leukemia is a cancer that doesn't originate in a tumor but in your blood, bone marrow, digestive tract, and lymphatic system.

There are chemotherapy drugs that are not cytotoxic but attack certain proteins.

Certain conditions that are not cancerous may require chemotherapy such as Crohn's disease, psoriasis, multiple sclerosis and lupus.

Chemotherapy may involve one drug (single-agent chemotherapy) or several drugs (combination chemotherapy or polychemotherapy.)

Although I will be detailing the psychological aspects of radiotherapy, not every cancer patient experiences this treatment. My father had chemotherapy for his cancer but he had no radiotherapy treatment. Most cancer patients get treated with a combination of chemotherapy, followed by radiotherapy (which is called chemoradiotradherapy.) Since this is the most common treatment for cancer, this is what I will be focusing on most in the book.

There are other forms of treatment but I will not be dealing with them because they are exceptionally rare and there are far too many to go into detail. There's target therapy, hyperthermia therapy, hormonal therapy, immunotherapy, and many more. These types of therapy are based off the location and grade of the tumor. I had to mention these briefly as I didn't want to misinform you with the idea that chemotherapy and radiotherapy are the only available treatments for cancer sufferers.

MY WIFE'S STORY

When I finished college, I moved in with my wife, Julie (who was my fiancée at the time.) My wife was having back problems for three months and it seemed to be getting worse. Almost every night, she would have to get up at 4am and go downstairs and sleep on the couch because of sharp shooting pains in her lower back.

As soon as I moved in, she suddenly started getting a weird tummy pain. It wasn't a normal tummy pain; the pain was lower than usual. At this point, I said, "Ok, Julie, something is wrong. You have had back pain for months and now you have a weird stomach pain. How many more months of pain are you going to put up with before you see a doctor? How long are you going to sleep on the couch for? Another three months? A year? Two years? It's not going to get better until you do something."

(In case you can't tell, I'm a big fan of tough love.)

So Julie went to the doctor and he did some blood tests and a scan. He told her to come back the week after for a follow-up appointment

Julie left the house at 730am. Her appointment was at 810am. Sadly, I wasn't with my wife when she was told the dreaded news. I wasn't there because NOBODY thought that the diagnosis was going to be so severe. Even when the doctor said, "I wish I could say it's good news but..." the first thing my wife said was, "Oh no, do I need tablets?" The idea of Cancer wasn't even in the back of her mind until he said, "I'm sorry, I really didn't think it was going to be this but... yeah, you have cancer."

He then told her that she had cancer of the womb and she needed surgery as soon as possible (she went under the knife eight days later.) He then started speaking in medical jargon and my wife's mind just switched off. She could see his mouth moving but she couldn't her the words because her mind had gone into a frenzy.

My wife and I watched a television movie about a woman's battle with cancer called The C-Word. The story is based off Lisa Lynch, a magazine editor who got diagnosed with breast cancer when she was only 28 in 2008. Julie said the scene where the doctor diagnoses the woman with cancer was EXACTLY how she felt. She said that movie freaked her out because it was so spot-on how a young woman reacts when she learns she has cancer.

Another accurate depiction of being diagnosed with cancer is the movie, 50/50, which stars Joseph Gordon-Levitt and Seth Rogen. It's based off a true story about a young man called Will Reiser who was suddenly diagnosed with a rare spinal cancer called schwannoma.

Gordon-Levitt's plays a 27-year old called Adam who is fit, healthy and goes running regularly. One day he starts suffering back pains so he sees a doctor. When the doctor diagnoses him with schwannoma, doctor tells him very coldly and matter-of-factly. My wife said this is also how you will be spoken to by doctors quite regularly. Even though cancer is life-threatening to you, to a doctor, it's just part of his or her daily routine.

My wife and I would recommend these films to anyone who has cancer or knows someone who is battling it. They are both based off real people so the films are not glamorized; they are very grounded in reality. The C-Word and 50/50 don't sugarcoat or exaggerate the experience. They just show it for what it is. They're not too scary though. They shouldn't freak you out too much. They both have an uplifting ending that isn't cheesy or unrealistic. T

You know what the weirdest thing is?
The tummy pain was because of her ovaries. But her back ache had NOTHING to do with her tummy pain. It was just a coincidence. If she only had a tummy pain, she most certainly wouldn't have gone to the doctor. That's the scariest thing. As my wife says, "Cancer is a sneaky, evil little thing that just hides

inside you and does untold damage without you even knowing until it's too late."

Okay. I've explained cancer. I've explained chemotherapy. I've explained radiotherapy. I detailed the exceptions. And I gave my wife's experience.

Now it's time to look at the psychological side to it all.

CHAPTER 1

MOST OF THE BATTLE
IS IN YOUR HEAD

My wife, Julie, lost her hair seventeen days after her first chemotherapy. That's pretty normal.

The average person tends to lose their hair in-between the first two to three weeks after they begin treatment. My wife lost clumps of hair but she had to shave it all off to make it look even.

Some people lose every single hair but that's rare.

As horrific as this was, she didn't wallow. Instead, she went back to work for the first time in months the day after her hair fell out.

I remember she got up at the crack of dawn, put on her headscarf and went downstairs to go to work.

As I came downstairs an hour later, I saw my wife sitting on the couch staring at the ground. She never went to work. I asked if she was okay.

This is what she said -

"I want to wear a headscarf because it's comfortable but I look like someone who has cancer.

But everybody knows I have cancer so I shouldn't care...but I don't want people to stare.

But they're going to anyway because everyone knows

So I should wear my wig because I look normal and feel confidant

But what become lopsided or start to come off and I won't notice but everyone else will and it will be obvious to everyone except me and I will be humiliated.

So I should just wear my hat

But I get really hot and sweaty and it makes my scalp uncomfortable.

So I should just wear my headscarf

But I don't want to look like someone with cancer... if I wear my wig..."

Cancer forces your mind to go through an unhelpful mental cycle. You can torture yourself with this mentality. It is a cycle with no answers.

In Julie's situation, through trial and error, she felt most comfortable wearing a hat. My friend's mum, Eleanor, lost her hair when she had cancer and she felt confident wearing a wig. My neighbor, Nora, thought a headscarf suited her best.

Each to their own. There is no one answer for everybody.

The problem that a lot of people will have is that they care what other people will think of them rather than how they feel themselves. You should wear what makes *you* feel comfortable, not others.

CHAPTER 2

THE UNKNOWN CAN BE WORST THAN THE WORST CASE SCENARIO

In Daniel Gilbert's book, Stumbling On Happiness, he discusses an experiment called Unpredictable Sudden Increases in Intensity of Pain and Acquired Fear. (It's exactly what it sounds like.) It demonstrates "what we don't know makes us nervous."

The study concluded that anticipating unpleasant events can minimize their impact. Volunteers in one study received a series of twenty electric shocks. They were warned that they were about to be shocked in three seconds each time.

Some volunteers were given a high shock twenty times.

Other volunteers were given three high shocks and seventeen low shocks. But the bizarre thing is that the volunteers who experienced the low shocks rated themselves as feeling more afraid than the volunteers who received high shocks. This is because the volunteers experienced different shocks at different times. They could never prepare for what was coming. The volunteers who only experienced high intensity shocks knew what was coming and adapted to it.

To quote Gilbert's book, "Three big jolts that one cannot foresee are more painful than twenty big jolts that one can."

Of all of the things my wife, worried about, the treatment that scared her the most was the chemotherapy. The first session was petrifying because she didn't know what to expect.

My friend, Esther's mother was battling cancer at the same time as my wife. She started chemotherapy one week earlier than Julie. Esther told me afterward that her mother reacted to it badly (as expected.) She was dizzy, vomiting, incredibly lethargic, and prone to intense aches in her bones and joints.

I dreaded telling Julie. I didn't want to sugarcoat it but I didn't want to scare her. In the end, I just told her what Esther's mother experienced. Julie's reaction was, "Great. Now that I know what to expect, I'm ready for it. It's going to be horrible but at least I know that for sure."

My friend, Frank, freaked out about her first chemo session. She had side effects afterward but they weren't that bad – nausea, headache, dizziness, fatigue. The next five sessions she had were far worse. She would suddenly need to be rushed to the hospital for a blood transfusion or to be attached to an oxygen mask because she couldn't breathe.

But here's the thing – she reacted to those sessions far better than the first one even though the first one was pretty tame. She dealt with the first session very badly simply because It Was The First Session.

My wife never had surgery before. She never stayed in a hospital in her entire life before she had cancer.

But now, she's been to hospital so many times for scans and check ups, that it feels normal." For most people, there is always a bit of tension when you enter a hospital. For my wife, the hospital stopped being a big event. It's just became a typical Tuesday morning.

CHAPTER 3

INFORMATION CAN BE YOUR GREATEST ENEMY

As soon as you know you have cancer, one of your first priorities is to learn everything about it. This is understandable but it can be self-destructive.

One of the first questions anyone will ask is, "What are my chances?"

How would you react if you found out your chances were 20%? Or 10%? Or less?

Would you go through the agony of chemotherapy, radiotherapy, injections, surgery, daily medication, bone and muscle aches, vomiting and nerve damage knowing that you still had a slim chance of surviving? It is completely understandable to say you don't want to go through all of that pain. Instead, you would want to enjoy what little time you have left with your family and loved ones.

But here's the thing; any chance is still a chance.

I know Lance Armstrong is no longer the beacon of hope that he once was. But despite his tarnished reputation, he can still be an inspiration. His doctor said he had a 25% chance of surviving testicular, lung and brain cancer. Armstrong thought that was good enough to push through and he did. He's been clear now for nearly twenty years.

But when Armstrong met the doctor that diagnosed him years later, the doctor told him that he lied when he told Armstrong that he had a 25% survival rate!

Lance Armstrong actually had a 3% survival rate!

But the doctor couldn't tell him that, knowing that it would be giving Armstrong a death sentence. If Lance knew the truth, he said he wouldn't have bothered to fight it. But that's the problem; too much information can count against you.

In this day and age, technology is too accessible. So it's nearly impossible not to research everything on the Internet. Years ago, you would need to look through medical books at your local library or counsel your doctor.

Nowadays, people will scour every website to understand the cancer they have. Doing this rarely ends well.

Photographs can be scarring.

Statistics can be traumatic.

Testimonies can be heart wrenching.

If you see the words "30% survival rate," that's how you will identify your cancer. That might be enough to see yourself as a "goner."

It depends on your mentality. I've seen people with a 1% survival rate who said that it was enough for them to try to beat it and they did.

One pupil from my primary school was given a 90% chance of survival when he was diagnosed with cancer.

But he didn't hear "90%." All he heard was "cancer." Sadly, he didn't couldn't deal with it and he took his own life.

So positivity can make a huge difference.

But there is one grave truth that you need to know about positivity.

Which brings me to my next point.

CHAPTER 4

A POSITIVE ATTITUDE ISN'T ENOUGH

The first person in my life to have cancer was my Uncle Jimmy, who I'm named after.

He died in July 1992 after a battle with stomach cancer. I was only six years old but I still remember him very well. I remember his voice perfectly and he looked so much like my father, I couldn't tell them apart sometimes.

He was one of those people who was easy to idolize because he seemed to have an uncompromiseable positive outlook in life no matter how bad things got.

He believed anything could be beaten with pure willpower.

When he was diagnosed with stomach cancer at forty-nine, he reacted very positively to it. He saw this as something he could conquer.

He had to take the train to Dublin every three weeks to go to the hospital for his chemotherapy. It was on the other side of the country and would take the whole day to go back and forth. It was a pretty exhausting journey for anybody, more so considering he was ill.

But he would joke about taking the train. He even called it The Chemo Train. He once bumped into one of his friends and asked what they were doing on the Chemo Train. That was his attitude. He wasn't going to crawl up into a ball and give up because of the cancer. He was going to beat it with a smile on his face.

After his treatment finished, he went to the doctor for a checkup. The doctor asked how he was feeling.

Jimmy said he felt fantastic. Chemotherapy is usually the most painful thing a human being will experience in his or her life so Jimmy couldn't believe how energized he felt.

The doctor told Jimmy that this was bad news. Chemotherapy kills cells; good cells and bad cells. Killing cells causes excruciating pain. If Jimmy experienced no pain, that means the treatment didn't kill any of his cells, cancerous or otherwise.

Jimmy never smiled again and barely spoke a word until his dying day, which was only a few days after. It was like his body gave up as soon as it realized he had no chance.

You can do everything right and the cancer can still get you.

But it works both ways. I know people who gave up, wallowed, said goodbye to everyone, made their peace with their friends, loved ones and God, put their affairs in order in terms of inheritance; and yet they pulled through.

A positive attitude is extremely important. But there's no guarantee. It's the most horrific truth in the world but not everything can be beaten. But that shouldn't stop anyone from trying.

CHAPTER 5

YOU WILL BE CONSTANTLY REMINDED THAT YOU HAVE CANCER

It's easy to assume that a person with cancer only talks and thinks about being ill.

But Julie and I would eat out, go to the cinema and prepare for our wedding by picking up our rings, looking at venues and meeting photographers. So a lot of the time, Julie was just living her life.

But every now and again, she would get a reminder.

One day, Julie and I were walking to a jewelry shop to get my wedding ring re-sized when two teenagers stopped walking and gawked at Julie. Julie had her headscarf on and the two boys probably had rarely seen a person with cancer before. Incidents like this were quite common. But when they occurred, Julie would say to herself in her head, "Oh yeah... I have cancer."

It was an inescapable reminder. Julie would be in the middle of chatting to her friends or playing with her niece and then something or someone will bring her right back to reality.

When her friends and family asked how she was feeling, they mean well. They are showing that they care about her well-being. But sometimes when she would be feeling good, a person asking about her health would remind her why she should be depressed. It always seemed to happen when she was starting to feel normal again. Not asking about the cancer can be as important as asking about it. When people didn't ask about her illness, it made her feel normal. She could gossip about work, chat among friends and talk about upcoming movies she wanted to see.

You can become so self-conscious of people on the street gawking at you and reminding you of your illness, that it's not uncommon or unreasonable for you to stay at home all of the time. No one can bother you there.

But there's a catch.

People going through treatment will have a lot of free time at home to recover and heal. So the most common pastime is watching television.

Julie and I regularly watched comedies or a romantic movie to stay positive.

But Julie would still be reminded that she was ill. No matter what movie or television show we'd watch, there would always be a character who is in hospital or who's ill or who just died or is about to. No matter what we watched, it felt like there was some reminder to taunt my wife.

Julie dealt with this in a constructive way. Instead of watching comedies to distract her from her illness, she watched a lot medical documentaries to educate and inspire her.

She watched a documentary about a young boy who had a degenerative spinal disease. He was given little chance of recovery but he pulled through. Documentaries like this lifted Julie's spirits up.

She watched another documentary of a girl with a gargantuan growth in her mouth. The doctors cut it out and the young girl went back to school and started to feel a semblance of normality for the first time in years.

But the growth returned at an aggressive speed and grew bigger than ever. It was so big that she couldn't even speak.

Tears would roll down her cheeks as she cried silently, staring at her helpless mother.

This documentary might terrify somebody in Julie's shoes. But she saw this young girl and thought, "I thought I was bad. She's only ten. She hasn't done anything yet with her life and what she's going through is fifty times worse than what I'm going through. After seeing this girl, I realized that things could be so much worse."

I admired my wife's mentality. She didn't ignore her illness but she didn't allow it to control her life. It's impossible to run away from your cancer. It's going to be the first thing people ask about you. Just accept it and find the most constructive mentality on how to deal with it. My friend, Seamus, tried to disassociate from his cancer but it only hurt him more. He was diagnosed with skin cancer two years. After his diagnosis, he wouldn't listen to music or watch television or catch up with his friends. He would just sit in a chair and think about his cancer.

He has recovered since (his chances were always quite positive) but he reacted very badly to it. He pushed everyone away because he didn't want people to remind him that he was sick. But locking himself in his house all day was constantly reminding him of what he was running away from.

I have constantly tried to be there for him but since he was diagnosed, I have never met him once since. He sends vague, cryptic texts but never rings or picks up the phone. If I mildly reference his illness e.g. "How are you?" he won't text back. He will send silly messages or funny jokes but won't respond to genuine concern. He's trying to distract himself from his illness but it actually makes him more aware of his illness. He's only hurting himself and the only thing all of his friends and family are trying to do is make sure he is okay.

CHAPTER 6

DON'T NEGLECT YOURSELF

Do you know what was the first thing my wife did when she was told she had cancer? She went back to her car and wrote a Goodbye Letter to me. She was diagnosed three years ago but she only told me that a few weeks ago. She said she didn't want to tell me because she was embarrassed. I found it reassuring because my father did something similar.

My father was an atheist. My father had always been an atheist since he was a child. My father was born in the 1940s and being an atheist in the mid-twentieth century was odd and rare in Ireland. When I went to church, everyone would head up to the priest at the end of Mass and be offered their Communion wafers which would represent the body of Christ. My father never joined us in this practice, which I found strange as a young child.

You see, my father lost his mother when he was only three years old. He couldn't understand why God would take a boy's mother away from him so his belief in a higher power never formed. He never bullied other people about their religious beliefs. On the contrary, my father developed a deep respect for all religious beliefs. He wished he could share that faith.

However, the very first thing my father did when he was diagnosed with terminal pancreatitis was go to confession. The following day, he told my mother about his diagnosis. Immediately after telling her of his terminal sentence, he said, "Before you say anything, I just want to let you know that I went to confession yesterday for the first time in my life. So you don't have to worry about me spiritually."

It's not uncommon for terminally ill atheists to find God at the last minute "just in case."

But that is not why my father went to confession. He did it because he didn't want my mother to worry about his soul when he was gone.

It shows how selfless human beings can be. Even when we are in our darkest hour, our intention is to alleviate other's mood, not our own.

My wife, Julie used to stress about how much pressure her illness was putting on me. She felt bad that she was leaving me alone if she died. She would talk about the idea of me remarrying after she was gone. The most heartbreaking thing she ever said was, "I don't want you to love me then lose me."

Being diagnosed with cancer is one of the only times in life you are entitled to wallow a little bit and my wife did anything but wallow.

But here's the thing. If you have cancer, don't worry about everyone else. Don't worry about work or bills or how people have to arrange their schedules do they can look after you.

Don't feel selfish. When you are ill, it's your job to rest. It's everybody else's job to look after you. If you stress about others, they will stress about you. This will create a negative cycle, which will benefit no one. If you are worried about bills, someone will pick up the slack. Work will understand. I believe the reason people act this way is so they can stress about anything EXCEPT the cancer. They don't want to face it. No one wants to face it.

But you have to. What choice do you have?

So don't worry about your family and loved ones. All they want to do is look after you. Let them do their job. Don't worry about others. Worry about yourself.

CHAPTER 7

YOU ACTUALLY HAVE TO READ DOCTOR FORMS

On a doctor's form, there is always one page where it asks if you have or ever had high blood pressure, diabetes, high cholesterol, allergies, family history of heart disease, etc.

The majority of people will glance at this and tick "No" for all of them. You might tick "Yes" for one of them and it will probably be for something minor like asthma, which you haven't had a problem with in years. You can complete this page in seconds.

But if you have any history with cancer, you have to read all medical forms thoroughly. You will probably have to do this for the rest of your life. It's freaky the first time you have to do this because you are so used to glancing at this page and not associating with any of the disorders. Heart disease, prostate disease, bronchitis are disorders that other people get, not you.

Then one day, you get ill, and then you become one of those people.

When my wife and I signed up to a new doctor recently, I zoomed through the medical form in minutes. Julie, however, took about a half hour.

This may sound like a minor point compared to the other chapters but this sort of thing can get to you. It can be pretty grating after a few years knowing that you have to read the medical form in detail EVERY TIME for years and years.

CHAPTER 8

BEING STRONG CAN COUNT AGAINST YOU

There is a disaster movie called The Core where the Earth's core has stopped spinning and they have to reactivate with it with a nuclear bomb. It's a typical silly Hollywood blockbuster.

To fix the core, they have to send the best of the best.

Hilary Swank's character, Beck, is the best driller in the world and she has never failed a job in her life. As she prepares to descend to the core, one of the characters says, "You think you're strong but nothing like this has ever been attempted. We have one shot. If you fail, everyone dies. I know you have never failed a job before but that means you have never learned how to deal with failure. Let's see how strong you are then."

I didn't think much of the line (or the movie) at the time. But years later, that line came back to me when my friend's father became ill.

My friend, Siobhan's father was diagnosed with prostate cancer. Siobhan said her father was a commanding man. He wasn't a big guy but he had a booming voice and a natural authority about him that allowed him to take charge of an entire room of people with minimal effort. Siobhan always saw him as the strongest person she ever knew.

Siobhan was away from home when she was told her father had cancer so when she went home to see him a few days later, she expected him to be pretty shaken up by it.

But she could barely recognize him. That unwavering authority her father always had was gone. He looked like a shell of the man he once was.

Her father was the manager of his company for decades. Everyone relied on him to take control of every situation and to fix everything, either professional, financial or personal. He had been strong for so long, he never learned how to deal with feeling weak. This was the first time he felt fear since he was a child, and so he reverted back to a child-like state where he felt like he needed his family to do everything for him.

At first, he thought he could beat the cancer the same way he achieved everything in life – willpower. Sadly, cancer doesn't work that way. It attacks you on a cellular level. Your body will go to pieces.

Siobhan's father was in his sixties. His generation wasn't known for talking about his feelings as openly as society is today. So for him to talk about his fear, his daily terror and his depression would overwhelm him. He would go into a shock and not speak for days.

Sadly, Siobhan's father eventually lost his battle with prostate cancer.

So being strong may not only be enough to beat cancer but it can actually go against you.

But it works both ways. Being weak can actually help you.

My friend, Donna, was a hypochondriac. She would freak out over the smallest illness to the point where the emergency line stopped taking her calls.

She was easily rattled in her life. A bad day at work could send her into a depression. She had a new boyfriend every month but when each one finished, she acted like it was the end of the world.

Two years ago, she was diagnosed with lymph node cancer. I assumed it would drive her over the edge.

But I was astonished how positive she was about it. She said to me, "I turned every insignificant thing into a drama, which made me fall apart over and over again. But I only fall to pieces because I know I can get back up.

But I can't let myself fall to pieces over this because if I do, I don't know if I can recover."

She was so used to feeling weak, she knew how to deal with it when the danger was real.

She dealt with all of her treatment very courageously. Usually she needed her friends to support her for a few weeks when she has a bad break-up and she would paste every detail all over Twitter and Facebook. But she got through her cancer almost entirely by herself.

You may see yourself as a strong person but being confident, successful, popular and admired is redundant when you know you can lose your life.

Anyone can feel vulnerable. Sometimes, the strongest thing a person can do is admitting that you can be weak.

CHAPTER 9

YOU WILL WANT TO GIVE UP

If you went for a run and you started feeling tired, a part of your brain will consider giving up. But you need to ignore that impulse and keep going. But if you keep running faster, the impulse to quit will become stronger as you grow more tired and dehydrated.

Eventually, you will reach a breaking point where you physically can't run anymore and you will have to stop. When this occurs, what's the worst thing that could happen? You might be a bit disappointed with yourself because you could have run faster or for longer or your last run was better. You may be annoyed because you want to get rid of some belly fat. That's that worst thing you can lose.

But when you fight cancer, you can't quit. It's not like giving up on a run where you will lose the chance to have a better body.

You will lose your life.

You will lose everything.

You will lose the chance to spend time with your loved ones and family and see your children grow up. You will lose the chance to grow old with your partner.

If you didn't exercise to your full potential, there's always next time. There is no "next time" with cancer. You have to fight it then and there. It's the hardest thing you will ever do but it happens to have the greatest prize – a second chance at life.

Professional runners will keep running until their body can do no more. They aren't doing it to stay alive. But you have to.

CHAPTER 10

THE SMALLEST THING CAN SEND YOU OVER THE EDGE

Five months into my wife's treatment, she was strongly considering to give up. At the time, Julie only had a week and a half left of radiotherapy. So after nearly six months, my wife was ready to pack it in with only a few days left.

You might think this is because my wife found the radiotherapy too hard. Although radio wasn't easy, Julie has said many times that she found chemotherapy and surgery far more traumatic.

But the radiotherapy was the straw that broke the camel's back. After being told she had cancer with no warning, she was expected to have emergency surgery the following week, then she had to stop working for months, then she had to go shopping for wigs and headscarves, then she started chemo, then she had to wait for her hair to fall out, then she had to adjust all of her plans around the fact that she was getting sick sporadically, then had to cancel all of her plans for the next couple of months for shows, plays, concerts, etc. and then she had to have radiotherapy.

While she is doing this, she has to constantly have checkups, scans, injections, tablets, blood transfusions and x-rays.

And while she is doing all of that, she was trying to prepare for our wedding. So every spare minute (which there was very few,) she would have look at veils and shoes and flowers and wedding dresses and organize venues and food, etc.

Organizing a wedding is one of the most stressful things a person will ever go through. I can't even conceive the level of stress Julie must've been under dealing with the wedding and her treatment simultaneously. It's no wonder she buckled under the stress during her radiotherapy. It's astounding that she lasted as long as she did before she even considered quitting.

If you are reading this and you are battling cancer, remember that the slightest thing can send you over the edge. Your darkest hour may come when you least expect it. I don't want to scare you by saying that. I just want you to be prepared for the worst. If you are reading this for the benefit of a loved one who's combatting cancer, I need you to be aware that your loved one may snap and react with anger or terror or depression. You would expect someone with cancer to be prone to lashing out. But it might happen when you aren't prepared for it. Hair loss or vomiting may not be the symptoms that send someone over the edge. It could be something as simple as dropping a cup of tea or running out of bread. I was putting my wife to bed when she suddenly started crying. I had absolutely no idea that Julie was so close to quitting until she collapsed into my arms, begging me not to take her to treatment the following day. She didn't say anything to me about it all day but obviously she was thinking about it a lot.

My way of convincing her to keep going was by saying, "Babe, there is only a few more sessions left and then you're done. I know you are so tired, so frustrated and you are in so much pain. But if you never want to go through this again, these next few sessions may make all of the difference. These next few days of radiotherapy may decide whether the cancer ever comes back or not. What if you quit your treatment and then you find out that the cancer has returned? Until your dying day, you will wonder if those last few sessions could have made all of the difference in the world."

Thankfully, my wife is an incredibly rational woman and she agreed with my logic. She continued with her treatment until the very end. To this day, she has been cancer free for over two years. I like to think it was those last few days that made all the difference.

CHAPTER 11

YOU CAN STILL HAVE A LIFE

I was staying at a Bed and Breakfast years ago in the Aran Islands off the coast of Ireland. One evening, I was talking to the owner. She told me that she was looking after her sister over the last two years after she got brain cancer.

The next morning, I saw a young woman running into the B&B. I'd seen her jogging around the island for the last few days. She was in her twenties, blonde and well-built. She said hello to me and we started chatting. I asked how long she was staying at the B&B for. She said that she wasn't a customer at the B&B. She lived there. Her sister owned the Bed and Breakfast.

It took me a moment to register that this was the woman with the brain cancer her sister had told me about. I didn't realize at first because I had an image in my mind of a bed-ridden woman, shriveled up looking like she was at death's door. This woman looked more fit than most of my gym-obsessed friends.

It must be so reassuring to see a woman like this defying stereotypes. This woman was seizing the day. And because of that, people won't associate her with cancer.

Most of my friends who knew my wife was ill had never met her. So they naturally associate images of her being weak and bed-ridden like I did with the woman at the B&B.

So on our wedding day, they were so surprised to see how energetic and... normal she seemed.

At our wedding, my wife made a speech where she referenced her battle with illness.

My friend, Dan, thought, "Oh yeah...forgot about that" because my wife looked so strong on that day. To me, this is one of the best compliments my wife could receive.

Your life doesn't have to become your illness. You can still have a life outside of it. Self-pity is a choice.

<u>CHAPTER 12</u>

LIFE CAN SEEM TRIVIAL

In 2006, my father was misdiagnosed with leukemia. His mentality was, "OK, I've led a good life. I've accomplished everything I wanted to do. I have no regrets."

But three weeks later, the doctor told him that it was a mistake and he was perfectly healthy.

For most people, this would feel like a second chance of life.

But my father sank into a depression because he was forced to face his own mortality. Facing your death can warp your perception of reality. If you accepted that you are going to die, your brain will gradually start to limit your priorities. Your hobbies would stop being a priority. Activities like television and movies would seem trivial. You may stop caring about politics, knowing that you won't be around to see how they shape the world. You won't be interested in what happens in the next season of your favorite television show because you won't be around to see it.

Eventually, your only priorities will become your family and loved ones.

Your mind starts limiting your priorities almost immediately after you acknowledge your life is coming to an end. So once my father realized he was fine, it was too late. His priorities had already shifted. He would see his favorite films as wasting two hours of his life when he should be seizing the day. He was too self-aware that his life on Earth was temporary. His end may not be for years but sometimes it's impossible to unthink what we have thought.

It's not like my father was prone to this sort of negative behavior. He got out of his depression after about a year.

But at some point, you will feel that triviality. You might be at home watching television just to pass the time when you will suddenly think, "I might die in the next few months and I'm spending my last moments on Earth watching some stupid comedy!"

What was once your biggest priority may become an insignificant concern once you are faced with your own mortality. In the last few months of my father's life, there was a presidential election in Ireland. Ireland was about to have its first new president in fourteen years. It was a huge deal. It was an even bigger deal because my father was a supporter of one of the candidates, Michael Higgins, for years. So my father was telling everybody to vote for Higgins.

And he won. Michael Higgins is the new president of Ireland. My mother was so happy that she told my father as soon as she could. But within the weeks between the election starting and finishing, that was one priority my father no longer had. He didn't care because he knew he wouldn't be around to see how Higgins would impact the country. All my father cared about at that time was his family.

If a loved one of yours is battling cancer and they seem to be disinterested in things that they used to be passionate about, it's important not to take it personally. It's not that they don't care anymore. Their mind is simply reprioritizing everything as best it can. The mind is simply making the best of an impossible situation.

CHAPTER 13

ONE DAY, IT WILL FEEL NORMAL

I had to go to the dentist last week. It is literally a twelve second walk from my house. And it took me two weeks to pluck up the courage to go because I was afraid of getting a filling. Why was I such a wimp? Because I haven't been to the dentist in years.

Why are people so scared of hospitals? Because hospital visits are far and between. Most people can go years, even decades between hospital visits.

My wife had to go to hospital over forty times in six months during her treatment. She has had surgery three times in the last two years. She never had surgery once before she was thirty. Until she was diagnosed, she never even stayed a single night in hospital. The idea of sleeping in a hospital ward was terrifying to her. On her last stay in hospital, her main gripe wasn't the fact that she was in hospital or she was having surgery; she was mostly annoyed because she couldn't get the right pillow!

When my wife was told that she need surgery for the third time, she didn't panic or have a tantrum. She just said, "But I have tickets to see Michael McIntyre at the O2!!! TYPICAL!"

(That isn't an exaggeration. My wife had tickets to see a comedian EVERY TIME she needed surgery at the last minute. She refuses to book another comedian. She's convinced that she's jinxed.)

You're scared when anything feels unfamiliar – going to a new school, having a child, starting a new job, moving house. But before you know it, everything becomes second nature. The first time you have to change a baby's nappy, it feels like the most terrifying thing in the world (and the most disgusting.) But within a few weeks, it's second nature (but still disgusting.)

As big as hospital treatment or surgery is, my wife dealt with it the same way; she got used to it. So if you feel like the constant hospital visits are tiring, depressing and overwhelming, just take it one day at a time.

Now she doesn't worry about the idea of needing more surgery.

She worries about needing more surgery in the middle of her next holiday!

Cancer feels like the end of the world at first. It seems patronizing when a doctor tells you that the treatment and the injections may seem scary but they will become second nature in a few months time.

But it's true. You will feel terrified at some point but it won't be permanent.

My wife got up one day and took her tablets. I gave her an injection to regrow her marrow cells in her bones, which had deteriorated from chemotherapy. This caused the worst pain of Julie's entire treatment. New cells growing too quickly in her bones created what my wife dubbed an intense "bone ache" which lasted for days.

Julie would then down a pint of water. It's vital to keep your fluid levels up when you have cancer. However, it will force you to go the toilet a lot which is frustrating because when you feel terrible the last thing you want to do is get up from your bed all day. It's extra tough to drink a pint of water because chemotherapy effects your taste buds so water usually taste like metal. Sadly, this symptom can last even after you finish your treatment. In rare cases, it can last a lifetime.

After Julie had her tablets, water and injections, we went to the doctors. Julie needed a blood test because she had a blood transfusion the previous week (on her birthday.)

We drove to the cinema to watch the James Bond movie, Skyfall. During the film, Julie had a horrific coughing fit because she was rundown. She felt like she was ruining the movie for everybody so she left the room for fifteen minutes. She came back once she felt better. She didn't miss much. (She hates James

Bond movies with a passion. She only watched this one because Adele did the theme song.)

When the movie was over, we went to the pharmacy so Julie could get anti-sickness tablets. We grabbed some dinner at a restaurant. Julie had two bites but gave up because the meat tasted like metal.

While we were driving home, I felt the day might have been a bit too much for Julie. I asked how she was feeling.

"Good," she answered. "I just can't wait for your family to finally meet mine at the wedding."

I corrected her by saying, "No, I meant how are you feeling about your treatment?"

She replied by saying, "Fine. I forget I have cancer most of the time."

That was the most reassuring thing she could have possibly said. Some people can get lost in all of the injections and tablets and hospital visits. But Julie was going through the motions on autopilot while she was focusing on practical things like our wedding.

There is nothing wrong with cancer "feeling normal." When you have that mentality, it means that you are not letting it control your life. It means you are not letting it identify you.

CHAPTER 14

YOU WILL FEEL ASHAMED

It's not uncommon for people to feel like they have done something wrong when they discover they have cancer. Society associates lung cancer with smoking; liver cancer with alcohol; stomach cancer with a bad diet.

So if you do smoke and you got lung cancer, it's easy to think that it's your own fault.

My old principal got nose cancer. He felt ashamed because he was so proud of how healthy he was. He couldn't understand what he possibly did wrong to deserve it.

If you have this mentality, get rid of it. You can't blame anyone, especially yourself. Even if your lifestyle did cause the cancer, don't try to punish yourself. That sort of mentality will destroy you. If smoking caused you to get lung cancer, then quit smoking and prepare to battle for your life.

Wallowing gives the cancer a chance to spread. Fight it.

This applies to anyone you know that has been diagnosed with cancer. You might have a friend who drinks a lot. One day, your friend may get liver cancer. There is never a time for "I told you so" or "I warned you but you didn't listen."

That's not helpful. That's not your job. As a friend, it is your duty to stand by their side and support them every way imaginable.

You might feel shame because you associate illness with weakness. This can be so much harder if you rarely feel weak. It will feel like an alien emotion.

What if you were a powerful manager of a company who is used to being in control and having to answer to nobody? How are you going to feel about missing important deadlines and business deals that you spent months on? How would you feel knowing that hundreds, maybe even thousands of people work underneath you and you are suddenly whisked away from all of that? Can you imagine going from that to needing help to get out of bed from a total stranger? That can shatter a person's self-confidence and perception of reality. One day you might see yourself as an unconquerable big shot; the next day, you need to ask the nurse to assist you putting on your hospital gown. A lot of people in this circumstance will desperately try to do everything themselves even when it is physically impossible.

They act like this because they are used to not needing people. But when you have cancer, everyone needs help. No exception.

This is one of the reason's why hospitals have the Pain Grade system. My father was an extremely proud man who didn't want to be a burden to anyone. So when we asked him how he felt, he just said, "Fine." That is a redundant answer. He's not fine. He's very ill. But we need to know how ill he feels.

A doctor doesn't say, "How do you feel?" They would say, "On a scale from 1 to 10, what level is your pain?"

Only then would my father give an answer. Obviously the Pain Grade system was formed to accommodate patients by giving him the appropriate amount of painkillers. But it also stops people from hiding their pain and stopping patients feeling ashamed about their struggles with the treatment.

If my father's pain was 1 or 8, he would just say he felt "fine" unless we used the Pain Grade.

Not only did the Pain Grade help us understand how bad his pain was, but it let him open up about his feelings. The conversation would go like this –

The doctor would say, "Where are you from 1 to 10?"

"9," My father would answer.

"Ooh. That sounds pretty serious."

"It was a 6. But it crept up on me over the last hour. I didn't realize how bad it was until you asked."

"Does that frustrate you?"

"Well sometimes it's so constant, I get used to it. Other times, it's so constant I am just sick of it. I'm scared that it's going to get worse. I can't imagine how it can be worse. But I know it will be."

That gave us a much better window into my father's mind than "Fine."

My wife acted similarly when I asked her how she felt. She would say "Fine" because she didn't want me to worry. But I worried more because I didn't know how she really felt.

Even when she was genuinely fine, I would still worry because I couldn't tell if she was just saying that. When I did the Pain Grade, I got a much better sense of her mental state. Every now and again, she would say, "I feel really good actually. This is the best I felt in weeks." That would mean so much more than "fine" knowing that it was genuine.

Even when she was upset and said, "I feel terrible. I don't know how I'm going to take anymore of this pain," I felt a little better because at least I knew how she felt and I hoped she would feel better letting that emotion out.

CHAPTER 15

IT PUTS EVERYTHING IN PERSPECTIVE

Stressed at work? Can't find a boyfriend or girlfriend? Having family troubles? Frustrated that you can't lose your belly fat?

All of your petty insecurities will vanish once you get diagnosed with cancer.

Do you know what my biggest priority and worry was before my wife was ill? Do you know what my wife and I were stressing about the day before she got diagnosed?

Maggots.

Maggots got in our bin outside our house and we were in bed on our phones trying to find the correct way to kill them.

That was our top priority.

The next day, Julie was diagnosed and the maggots became a very distant priority. You kill them with boiling water in case you were wondering.

People can become extremely stressed about work or bills or rent or mortgages or relationships and we can overdramatize them. But if someone close to you becomes ill, it can help you put your life into perspective.

I've always noticed the people who have the biggest problems deal with them better than people who have no problems.

My friend, Saorise, had a really hard time when she was young. Her father suffered a stroke when she was fifteen. The stress of it was so intense that Saorise's mother had a nervous breakdown the next day. Over the years, Saorise's father has had four strokes in total, each one worse than the last.

Saorise had to look after both of her parents every day for years. She had to become their carer while simultaneously doing her exams at school.

Saorise is one of the nicest people I have ever met in my life. You can't say a bad word about her. I have probably never met a human being better at dealing with stress than her.

I know someone else called Robin. (I can't say I'm friends with this person) She only talks about herself and is one of the most self-absorbed people I have ever known. She is obsessed with two things, her appearance and boys. By the way, she has never had a boyfriend in her life.

But one day, Robin's best friend, Lora got skin cancer on her face. If this happened to any other woman, it would be horrific. But it was even more devastating to Lora because she was a model. She knew her career was finished.

But over time, Lora was just happy to be alive. It was a horrific incident but it gave Lora some perspective. Although she will never look the same, her appearance is not the end of the world.

You'd think this incident would've given Robin some perspective…. you'd really think that, wouldn't you?

But she never changed. She seems worse than ever.

The problem Robin has is that whatever self-created problems she has, she never realizes that there are other people who are going through far worse.

Which reminds me…

CHAPTER 16

THERE IS ALWAYS SOMEONE WORSE

Julie found radiotherapy tedious. This treatment is comprised of twenty-five sessions. Chemotherapy tends to have six sessions. Julie nearly quit her treatment entirely near the end of radiotherapy because it was so tiring. I asked her to give it one more day, hoping it would change her mind.

When she went into the hospital the next day, she saw a man who was at least eighty years old. His whole body looked like it was ready to fall apart. We noticed this guy came every day alone. He had no friends, family, children or carers to bring him back and forth to the hospital.

After Julie finished her session, we walked back to our car and we saw the same man walking to his. We assumed he was getting a lift from a taxi, ambulance, friend or a care home.

We were wrong. He drove to the hospital alone every single day.

I don't know what happened to that man but I believe it is safe to say that he had little to no chance of survival. Even if he did survive, I don't know what he would be living for since he doesn't seem to have any friends or family.

Nevertheless, this man still found the strength to go for his treatment every single day.

That gave my wife some perspective. She said to me, "He has no one to fight for except himself but he is still fighting everyday. If he dies, it won't effect anyone else. If I die, it will destroy my family." That mentality gave Julie and extra incentive to push through with her treatment.

CHAPTER 17

RADIOTHERAPY CAN BE WORSE THAN CHEMOTHERAPY

After three months of chemotherapy, patients will normally have a break for three or four weeks before they start radiotherapy.

Radiotherapy usually consists of five sessions per week for five weeks, each one lasting for approximately fifteen minutes. A laser will be fired at the cancer cells. After enough exposure to the laser, the cancer should slow down, go into remission, or die. Since chemotherapy is meant to be the worst part of the treatment, it can be such a relief once it is over.

But you are not out of the woods yet. Radiotherapy is another hurdle you need to jump over. In a nutshell, chemotherapy is painful; radiotherapy is tiring.

Chemotherapy is awful but you have three weeks to recover for the next one.

Radiotherapy makes you lethargic. But there's no break. You have to go again the next day. And the next day. And the next day.

And just as you are barely starting to regain your strength during your two free days per week, you realize that you have another month of this relentless treatment.

The tiredness you experience from radiotherapy isn't the same type of tiredness you experience from a lack of sleep.

You know when you have an intense workout in your legs, and the next day your lower body is aching so much that it takes effort to do the simplest tasks like climbing a stairs? Now imagine that level of exhaustion in every part of your body. Now imagine you have to drive to the hospital yourself every day for five weeks.

I have only met one person that found radiotherapy worse than chemotherapy. But I don't want you to get into a false sense of security. Just because the chemo is finished doesn't mean the battle is over. Believing that the worst is passed and all that is left is the homestretch can be a damaging mentality. Expecting a lot of pain and receiving it may not be as bad as receiving a little bit of pain but not expecting it.

<u>CHAPTER 18</u>

YOU WILL FIND A STRENGTH WITHIN YOU TO KEEP GOING

My mother's best friend, Ann, was diagnosed with breast cancer eleven years ago.

Ann is one of the most religious people I have ever met. She's incredibly old-fashioned and set in her ways. She tries to live the purest life possible.

If my mother was available while Ann was having her treatment, she would drive Ann to the hospital for injections, chemotherapy and radiotherapy. But my mother was often busy working so most of the time, Ann would have to go to the hospital herself.

She didn't have a car. She would cycle for miles to the hospital every day for six months. And every day, without exception, she went to church.

I have no idea how a woman in her fifties could have that much physical strength when she was going through the biggest battle of her life. It doesn't actually seem physically possible for her to possess such stamina. I asked her how she kept going.

Her answer was simple, "God."

Even if you are an atheist, it's impossible to argue with her. One of my atheist friends, Darragh said to me, "The one place no one ever makes fun of God is in a hospital." If that's what keeps her going, I can't argue with the results.

Ann has been clear for eleven years now. Religion was her fuel. It kept her strong. Everybody needs to find something to keep them going. It can be anything. You would be astonished what can fuel you. Let's look at another example.

My friend, Bob, reacted horrifically when he found out he had skin cancer. He described himself as being in "utter turmoil." His brother, Tomas, had fallen out with him years ago so Bob saw this as an opportunity for the siblings to forgive and forget.

But Tomas refused. He wanted to keep the petty feud alive and shunned his brother in his hour of need. Tomas actually said he couldn't care if his brother lived or died.

This could've resulted in Bob falling apart even further.

But it didn't. It helped him. Because Tomas refused to support his brother, Bob converted all of his fear and anxiety into a seething rage. This doesn't sound healthy, but anger is a fantastic driving force.

Many people throughout history have accomplished incredible things just to prove someone else wrong.

Bizarrely, after Bob had this argument with his brother, I never saw him feeling weak and depressed for the duration of his treatment.

Instead, he was strong and driven because of his rage. He would say to me he was doing this to prove he doesn't need his brother. Again, that may not sound like the soundest motivation. But if it works, it works. He got through his treatment and has been clear of cancer for five years now.

Find what motivates you. Ask what you are most passionate about. Harness that passion and convert into the fuel you need to get through hard times. You might think that you don't have that strength. You might see yourself as a wimp or someone who goes to pieces over the smallest thing.
Well, let's look at it this way. Everybody knows a person that went to pieces after they got dumped. I have a friend that took his break-up so badly, that he got heavily addicted to cocaine and horse tranquilizers and had to go to rehab.

This type of reaction doesn't only happen to people who are timid, weak-willed, immature, naïve or young. Anyone can be devastated by a break-up and react badly.

But when you see people battle life-threatening diseases or cancer, you think, "How can a person fight cancer for months or even years but there are some people who can't even deal with a break-up?"

But there's a very good reason why people with cancer deal with the relentless onslaught of pills, injections, surgery, treatment and countless side effects. It's not just because they are strong.

It's because their mind doesn't get a chance to psychologically register all of the horrific things that are happening. Cancer consumes your life for months, even years. That is too big to register and if you did, it would overwhelm you.

After my wife began her treatment, the nurse asked her a few days later to take three steps. She said, "No."

I could see in her eyes that she believed that there was no way she could possibly take three steps. It was like asking her to jump to the moon.

But after a lot of coaxing, she eventually got out of bed. It took all of her willpower to walk three steps. It was so much effort; it didn't seem possible to take a single step further.

But she did it. And that's a good start. But what's more important, is that the next day, she could walk seventy steps.

Every time she felt like she couldn't handle the pain or felt like she couldn't stand for another second, she would cast her mind back to that moment when she believed she couldn't take three steps.

When you experience the agony of chemotherapy or the fatigue of radiotherapy, you will want to quit. You might convince yourself that some people are strong enough to beat it and you are not one of those people.

But nobody finds cancer treatment easy. The most positive person in the world will have doubts and they will experience anger and frustration like anyone else. Everyone reacts badly. So if you know someone who beat cancer and they have been clear for years, you need to remember that they didn't beat it because they are stronger than you. Every human being is stronger than they believe. Everyone has more endurance and more stamina than they imagine. Cancer will take you to that threshold and you're only choice is to push through it.

Focusing on little victories like that can get you through the day. You can deal with the bigger picture after the treatment is over. You will have to.

__CHAPTER 19__

YOU WILL NEED TO KNOW A LOT ABOUT YOUR FAMILY HISTORY

As soon as you get diagnosed, the doctor will need to know everything about your family and what illnesses they are prone to.

My friend Bob (who I mentioned in the previous chapter) had skin cancer. After he got diagnosed, he went back to his doctor so they could discuss his treatment. Bob wanted to go alone but his mother insisted that she should be there too. Thank God she did.

The doctor asked Bob if there was any skin cancer in the family. He said no.

His mother corrected him by saying both his grandparents had skin cancer, his father had it years ago and her own brother died from it.

Only then did Bob realize how utterly clueless he was about his own family and the illness that could kill him.

Bob may sound ignorant or naïve but many people will find themselves in similar circumstances. Do you know what illnesses your family is prone to? It's not exactly an easy topic to bring up at any time, is it?

People only try to find answers to these questions when it is too late.

It can help to find out as soon as possible. It can even save your life.

Twelve years ago, my father noticed a mole on his arm was getting bigger and darker. This is a potential sign to skin cancer. Since he knew this was a common from of cancer in his family, he played it safe and had it removed.

My mother saw it as a waste of money but my father thought he couldn't put a price on his health.

A year later, the mole grew back. My father didn't give it a chance to grow and had it removed again.

My mother was furious. She said, "You spent HOW much money to remove a dot????"

A year later, the mole returned but this time, it turned malignant. They carved it out in time and my father recovered. The doctors said my dad was lucky because it was growing slowly. Moles like this can grow at incredible speed but having it removed twice seemed to have slowed it down.

My father's paranoia saved him. But to him, it wasn't paranoia, it was common sense.

I have a mole on my hand. I've had it since I was a child. But it's unchanged for twenty-four years so I am not paranoid about it.

But I am aware of it. I am aware that it might grow or get darker and if it does, it's not paranoid to check it out with a doctor. It's common sense.

CHAPTER 20

YOUR FRIENDS AND FAMILY GO THROUGH IT TOO

You don't suffer through the cancer alone. It affects everyone else around you.

But at least they can be strong when you can't be. When my wife was ill, her family and friends each found a different job to help her get through it.

Some people were there to make her laugh.

Others had been through the same battle and would give my wife empathy, which made her feel less alone.

Her married friends would talk about our upcoming wedding to help her focus on something positive.

Her co-workers were giving her the gossip about people at work.

I gathered as much information as possible. Some of the information was positive, which would uplift Julie and some of it was negative, which if I told her, could force her into a spiraling depression.

I needed to be careful how I filtered this information to her without sugarcoating it. Sometimes, her friends would try to say something constructive but it would make her feel worse.

I'll give you an example. Julie was only thirty when she was diagnosed. Therefore, the most common comment she would receive is, "Thank God you're young. You have youth on your side. You see elderly women beating cancer when they're seventy. If they can do it, you DEFINITELY will."

But there's a problem with this logic. The younger you are, the faster and more efficiently your cells grow.

Cancer isn't a disease. Cancer is made of your own cells. Which means the younger you are, the faster the cancer spreads.

Ian McKellen was in his sixties when he was diagnosed prostate cancer. He's had it now for about ten years but it's growing so slowly, that it's practically unnoticeable in almost a decade.

Julie's cancer on the other hand, went from Stage 1 to Stage 3 in two days.

So all of your friends and family need to learn what to say and what not to say. The most common instinct people have is to give advice. Advice has nothing but good intentions but it normally comes across as patronizing.

Saying, "I know how you feel because I felt the same way when I went through it" may seem helpful but it doesn't make the pain or fear go away.

I personally would never say, "I know how you feel." Everyone processes cancer in their own way. You can never know how someone feels, even if they had the same cancer as someone else.

The best thing to do is also the easiest thing – Just be there. Hold their hand when they need to concentrate on something besides the pain. Give them a hug when they feel like the whole ordeal is too overwhelming. When Julie was frustrated, it was naturally my instinct to try and say something reassuring but I usually suppressed that impulse and just gave her a hug. It seemed to calm her down much more than any advice. Advice usually worked her up into a frenzy.

Just being there doesn't sound like much but it means everything when someone is fighting for their life.

CHAPTER 21

YOU WILL FEEL ALONE

Even though one in three people statistically experience cancer at some point in their life, every person who's diagnosed with it will feel alone and isolated. You will see other people living their lives, having fun, getting drunk and partying and it can make you feel bitter and resentful because you can't take part in those activities.

When you realize that you are not the only person going through this, it can give you the drive you need to push through. My father and my neighbor, Nora, were battling cancer simultaneously. They were there for each other to make sure they saw their treatment to the end.

When my father wanted to quit his treatment, Nora would come to my house and talk to him, but more importantly, she would listen. When she heard how frustrated my father was, she would say, "I feel the same way... but I know I have to do it. What's the alternative?"

The following week, Nora would have her chemotherapy and come over to our house to see my dad and she would say, "Forget what I said! I was wrong! It's too hard. Too painful. It's impossible. How does anyone get through this?!!!"

By this point, my father was no longer feeling the symptoms of chemotherapy (they wear off after a week or so.) So now the shoe was on the other foot.

My father would say, "Nora, look at me. I feel fine now. You feel horrible but you will be okay by next week. I need you to feel okay next week because if you don't, who's going to stop me from quitting chemotherapy when I feel like you do now?!!"

This was great advice because it gave Nora extra incentive. She had to stay strong to support my father when he fell apart. If she gave up, so would my dad.

Although my father didn't recover, Nora did. She said she would've quit if it wasn't for my him. She saw it through because my father reminded her that she wasn't alone.

<u>CHAPTER 22</u>

CHEMOTHERAPY ISN'T ALWAYS PURE AGONY

Chemotherapy has a reputation for being the most painful thing a human being can experience. But it isn't that simple.

If your cancer is terminal, doctors may give you a larger dose of chemical compounds to give you an extra couple of months or years. A larger dose will kill more cancer cells but it will also kill many of your normal cells. This compound is filtered through your bloodstream so it can get to every organ in seconds killing as many cells as possible, whether they are good or bad.

My neighbor, Joe, had lung cancer. The mortality rate is incredibly high for lung cancer so he had to experience the unimaginable pain we associate with chemotherapy. Joe described the pain as such, "It's like the worst toothache you've ever had in your life, but it's in every part of your body. Your ears, the back of your eyes, your fingernails, in-between your toes.

And it's just a constant pain for about three days. And when it passes, you know you have to do it again and again."

Many cancer sufferers give a similar description when they are trying to make people understand what the pain is like.

One good mentality to have in order to help you get through the pain is – The more pain you are in, the more cancer cells the chemo is killing.

But this agonizing pain is derived from one chemical compound of chemotherapy. There are four chemical compounds involved with chemo. If you don't receive this compound, you will not experience this intense agony. You will experience nausea and fatigue but not everybody will go through pure agony. The doctors will tell you which symptoms you will experience and which ones you won't. The worst pain my wife experienced during the chemo was an intense bone ache. However, that ache wasn't directly from the chemo. As I mentioned in a previous chapter, the chemotherapy withered marrow cells in my wife's bones. I had to inject her with steroids that would make her bone cells grow at an astronomical rate. But because the cells grew too fast, they would be leave my wife in pain. I had to give her a foot massage three times a day to pull the sensation. Although she said the pain was intense, she said she was lucky she didn't go through the agony that some people like Nora or Joe or my dad went through.

CHAPTER 23

YOUR HAIR DOESN'T NECESSARILY FALL OUT DURING CHEMOTHERAPY

Chemotherapy is usually compromised of six sessions spread over three months. Chemical compounds will be inserted into your bloodstream to kill cancer cells. You will experience side effects over the next three of four days. Some people experience the symptoms within hours. These side effects include nausea, dizziness, backache, spasms, nerve damage, migraines, lethargy, vomiting, cramps, constipation and diarrhea.

Hair loss tends to happen in the first fourteen to twenty-one days.

After about two weeks of your first chemo session, your hair will fall out in clumps. Some people lose patches of hair. Others lose all of it.

From your first chemo session, you will start to lose the rest of your body hair over the next three or four months. This happens so slowly you may not even notice. Then suddenly, you'll notice that when it rains, water keeps getting into your eyes for some reason and that's when you may realize that you don't have any eyebrows or eyelashes.

Your hair will grow back thicker than before. It will probably not return exactly the way your hair was in terms of color or type (straight hair can become curly) but it should come back so you will need to be patient.

Despite what many people believe, losing your hair during chemotherapy isn't a guarantee. One of the compounds makes you lose your hair. If you don't receive it, your hair won't fall out. The doctors will know if your hair will fall out or not and they will tell you before you start treatment.

Your hair may become thinner as your body becomes weaker and you are not having sufficient nutrients but it will not fall out if you don't receive that specific chemical compound.

CHAPTER 24

LOSING YOUR HAIR CAN BE THE WORST PART

Whether or not your hair falls out can affect your life dramatically. My father had a specific type of pancreatic cancer called annular pancreatitis. It's the most lethal cancer in the world and the fastest killing.

But he didn't lose his hair. So people would speak to him normally, even if they knew he was ill, which was nice and reassuring for him because it made him feel normal.

But you may get a cancer that is treatable where your chances of recovery are high and you respond to the treatment positively but people will look at you like a zoo animal because you lost your hair.

Not everybody has a strong relationship with his or her hair. I lost my hair when I was twenty-two. I know it's not as bad for men but I know some guys who sank into depression once their hair started to fall out or recede.

Nevertheless, having a strong relationship with your hair is not the reason why losing it can be so devastating when you are going through chemotherapy.

There will always be someone who thinks, "It's just hair. It doesn't do anything. It could be worse."

Losing your hair is arguably the biggest psychological factor of cancer and with good reason. Losing your hair is the most noticeable part of the treatment.

Once you lose it, people will stare at you. Every time they stare at you, it reminds you that you have something inside of you that can kill you. So whether or not you have a strong relationship with your hair, that constant reminder can eat at you.

But you don't just lose your hair. As soon as you discover you have cancer, you know that there will be treatment, hospital trips, tablets, injections and possibly surgery.

Your body will probably start going through lots of changes. You may have reactions or allergies from your medication or because your immune system has been weakened.

You probably won't be able to eat enough and whatever you do eat will probably be vomited up later. Your body won't be able to break your food down as efficiently and it's likely you will experience diarrhea or constipation.

So by the time you lose your hair, you won't look like yourself with a shaved head. You will look tired and gaunt. Your skin will be extremely pale. Your eyes may be bloodshot from a lack of sleep. Your nails may appear discolored. You will probably lose your eyelashes and eyebrows at some point. You will barely recognize the person staring at you in the mirror. You will look really, really ill. You will look like someone that could die.

That's why losing your hair can be the worst part. When you look in the mirror for the first time after your hair falls out, that's when people tend to truly acknowledge the severity of the situation. No matter how positive you are as a person or how good you are at keeping your emotions in check, this is the most common time for people to have doubts that they can beat it. This is when people tend to fall apart.

But that's okay. Sometimes it's good to fall apart so you can put yourself back to together again and become stronger than ever.

When Julie lost her hair, she was horrified. But it wasn't wallowing; it was acknowledgement. It was acceptance. In a way, it was good to get it out of the way. That is the day that cancer survivors seem to dread more than almost anything. Once it comes and goes, they tend to just move on with the rest of their treatment.

<u>CHAPTER 25</u>

YOU WILL BE SCARED OF THE PAIN BUT THE MENTAL SIDE IS MUCH WORSE

What is the worst physical pain you ever experienced? I want you to really think about it. A broken bone? Childbirth? Dislocation? Nerve damage? Surgery?

Now I want you to visualize yourself reliving that pain. Try to get into the mind set you had at the time. Remember what you were thinking while you were experiencing that agony.

Now ask yourself – is that the worst thing you have ever been through?

A few months ago, my wife has recently had her gall bladder removed after she learned that she had gallstones (in case you can't tell, my wife hasn't had a lot of luck over the last few years.) A gallstone moving through your body is one of the most painful experiences a human being can endure. The nurses told me that it is more agonizing than childbirth. My wife said it felt like she was being stabbed over and over again from the inside for hours. When she was asked what level the pain was, she said it was a 10. It was unbearable. Even after she was given the most powerful painkillers, she said it felt like she went twenty rounds with Mike Tyson.

By the way, this happened on Valentine's Day.

That was without doubt and by far, the worst pain my wife has ever experienced. It was so horrible to see her in so much blinding pain that I still get upset thinking about it. I feel upset now just writing about it.

However, when I mentioned this to Julie, she said, "But that was ages ago! I'm fine now!" She is the one who went through the pain and she can get over it better than I can.

But how? How can she get through one of the most excruciating pains imaginable? Because when a pain is so unbearable, you don't have time to think about anything. You can't think about the future or the consequences. All you can think about is the pain.

The worst pain I ever experienced was when I experienced pharyngitis while on a ten-hour flight to Korea (the good Korea.) My throat closed up and by the time I got off the plane, I had to be rushed to hospital. The doctors didn't know what was wrong with me. Pharyngitis is such an obscure disorder that they couldn't make an educated guess what it was. So they just assumed it was Swine Flu (this was back in 2009 when Swine Flu was still a thing.) They injected me with the wrong drug which made it even worse. I remember the pain was so bad, I genuinely didn't care if I lived or died. I thought I did die when I blacked out from the pain. When I woke up, I was totally fine.

I barely remember that now. When I think of Korea, I think about the food, the people, the entertainment and spending time with my family. I forget about the minor inconvenience I had when I was quarantined in a Korean hospital wing where a doctor kept shoving different needles into my side (but it's a hell of a dinner party story.)

Nowadays, I don't give it much thought.

But I never stop thinking about my father's battle with cancer. Or my neighbors'. Or my uncle's. Or my wife's.

As I write this now, my wife had her 2 ½ year all-clear yesterday. When a cancer sufferer is cancer free for two years, the chances of the cancer returning plummet by 80%.

Although that is great news, there is residual mental damage lingering in the back of our minds.

But the worst part wasn't the pain. It was the unknown, the waiting, the side-effects, the effect it had on her job, cancelling on friends because she had to buy wigs, watching television to pass time and pretend you are not waiting to see when your hair is going to fall out.

The pain wasn't the worst part.

There was no worst part.

It was everything.

When the doctor asked Julie how painful her chemo was, she said it was an 8 out of 10. This is considered an intense ache. Not unbearable agony, just a dull lingering pain.

So why is an 8 out of 10 worse than a 10 out of 10?

Well, when you were in school, do you remember how impatient you would get waiting for a grade? Remember how irritated you would get waiting to see whether you failed or not? Now instead of waiting a few days, imagine waiting half a year. Instead of waiting for a bad grade, imagine waiting to experience agony that leaves you bed-ridden.

In the six months of treatment Julie experienced, she felt that level of pain for two months. That's 60 days out of 180. Do you know what that means? The only thing worse than pain is waiting for it. And Julie had to wait for 120 days. Julie had to meet friends, go to work, go about her day while she was trying to keep her mind off the inevitable pain, the inevitable side effects, the inevitable blood transfusions, etc.

At this point, I'm sure I'm making it sound like the scariest thing imaginable.

But no. I'm showing you how you can trap yourself into the worst kind of mental state. Look at it this way. You can't do anything about the pain. You CAN do something about how you react to that pain.

Chemotherapy has a nasty stigma as "the worst pain you will ever experience." Not everyone will experience it. Some people will experience symptoms like fatigue and nausea rather than intense agony.

But because of chemotherapy's reputation, it can affect you psychologically. When you start your treatment, you officially begin Your Battle Against Cancer.

The first time the nurse places a drip in your vein and you have watch the chemical compounds flow through the tube into your body can be a lot to take in. Knowing that drip is going to make your hair fall out and force you to experience intense pain for the next three months is enough to bring you to tears. It nearly always happens in the first chemo session.

My friend, MacGearailt, had chemotherapy after he was diagnosed with rectum cancer. When he had his first chemo session, he was excited that this treatment would make him better. But when the side-effects kicked in, he found the pain unbearable. He begged his family to stop the treatment but they said he had to continue. He was a nervous wreck every time he had to go back to the hospital for another chemo session.

His family said the doctors lowered his dosage so he didn't experience the same pain for his remaining sessions. However, the first one was such a shock to his system that he associated his chemo days with agony and terror.

It can work both ways. Julie was petrified on the day of her first chemo session. She did lose her hair and she was very upset about it but she didn't experience intense pain; just nausea and fatigue.

So she was terrified on the first day of chemo but eventually her mentality became more and more positive. The more chemo sessions she had, the more cancer cells were being killed. The whole experience made me realize something – The chemotherapy will effect you mentally no matter what. So make sure it effects you constructively and positively.

<u>CHAPTER 26</u>

YOU DON'T NECESSARILY LOSE A LOT OF WEIGHT FROM CHEMOTHERAPY

There are many reasons why you can lose weight from chemotherapy. If you have cancer in your pancreas, liver or stomach; eating will exasperate the cancer and cause intense pain.

Your body won't be able to break the food down efficiently because you are battling for your life.

Whatever you eat, it is likely you will vomit it up shortly after.

Another reason people tend to lose weight during treatment is because of the side effects from chemotherapy alters your taste buds. A lot of food will taste like metal (especially water.) You can't avoid drinking water because you need to stay healthy (especially during the radiotherapy phase.)

What's worse is that the metal-taste phase isn't necessarily temporary. There are some foods you can love for your whole life but they can taste metallic once you start chemotherapy.

But the original taste doesn't necessarily revert back to normal once the treatment ends. The taste might change for years, maybe ever for the rest of your life. After Julie finished her treatment, water tasted normal again. But Julie couldn't eat spicy chicken (her favorite food) for two years. The taste came back eventually (thankfully.)

During chemo, a lot of people will eat just enough food to get by. There is only so many mouthfuls of metal-tasting food a human being can manage.

However, losing a lot of weight isn't a guarantee from the treatment. When you are ill, you will not be able to do any intense exercise. Walking upstairs can drain you to the verge of collapsing.

You are going to spend a lot of time sitting on your couch, watching television or sleeping in your bed.

Since physical hobbies like going out, exercising, partying, meeting your friends and travelling are now limited, they are often replaced with another pastime – eating.

Your body will be so tired that your body will be craving carbohydrates to give you energy. So if you sit on a couch all day eating crisps and biscuits, you are going to gain weight, not lose it.

If you are a sporty and athletic person and you suddenly stop exercising, your muscles shrink and your fat grows faster than an average person.

This will only happen to certain people. But I do need to establish that losing weight is not a guarantee. Some people maintain the same weight and some people pile on fat.

CHAPTER 27

YOU WILL FIND OUT A LOT ABOUT ALLERGIES (AND YOU MIGHT EVEN DEVELOP NEW ONES)

After you are diagnosed, doctors and surgeons will ask if you have any allergies. When a person is asked if they have any allergies, he or she will usually say no without the slightest hesitation. But most people have never had an allergy test.

Even if you have had an allergy test, you may not have had one for years. Allergies can develop over time.

The doctors asked my wife if she had any allergies to medication and my wife said no. But my wife has never had surgery or strong painkillers before.

After her operation, the doctors gave Julie some morphine to relieve her pain. But she had an allergic reaction from the painkiller and was suddenly struggling to breathe.

This is terrifying for anybody but the doctors have dealt with this sort of thing countless times. They see patients who don't know what they are allergic to so they have certain protocols for this sort of situation. They remained calm and countered the morphine by filtering it out of her system and giving her penicillin.

However, Julie was allergic to penicillin as well. Her heart started pounding as if she was about to have a heart attack.

The doctors quickly intervened by giving her another painkiller called codeine to relieve her pain.

But she was allergic to that too! For her entire life, Julie was under the impression that she had no allergies. In reality, she was allergic to the three most effective painkillers.

In the end, all the doctors could give her was the most primitive painkillers like ibuprofen and paracetimol.

Not knowing what you are allergic to can kill you. Even Bruce Lee, a person many regarded as the fittest man alive, died from an allergic reaction to a muscle-relaxing painkiller.

Many people inaccurately believe that Bruce Lee died because he was allergic to aspirin. The drug he took is called Equagesic, (which is an aspirin) but Bruce Lee wasn't allergic to aspirin.

He was allergic to meprobamate, an ingredient in this type of aspirin. I may sound like I am splitting hairs but this sort of misunderstanding is exactly what led to Lee's death. He knew he had no problems with aspirin and had taken anti-inflammatory medication many times as he recovered from injuries during his fighting scenes.

But he had never taken Equagesic before and was oblivious that it was composed of an ingredient that was lethal to him.

And that was Bruce Lee! That guy could take down somebody twice his size with no problem. Bruce Lee was killed by something as anti-climatic as an allergic reaction when he was only thirty-two years of age. This is why people need to take allergies seriously.

Some people can get new allergies because of age, stress or illness.

I met up with my old principal from school recently for a catch up. He was a vegetarian who always looked after himself and prided himself in having a healthy lifestyle.

But he suddenly got a horrific nasal infection and he went to the doctor. The doctor told him he was allergic to nuts. He said that it was impossible because he ate nuts regularly and had never had a problem.

The doctor explained to him that you can eat something everyday for years and wake up one morning and suddenly become allergic to it.

It turns out his nasal infection wasn't an infection. It was cancer of the nose.

He has since developed other allergies. He used to live a carefree life but now, for the first time in his life, he felt paranoid. He gets frustrated because his friends think he has become a hypochondriac. They'll say things like, "Oh come on! Eat some nuts! You ate them for years. You can't suddenly be allergic to them!"

He has had full-blown arguments with his friends because he was so pedantic with how he eats and how he has to check everything that goes into his food. He has to make his own meals and rarely will eat at a café or restaurant unsure of what may be in his meal.

I would recommend everybody to get an allergy test. Even if you had one when you were a child and you think you know what your allergies are (or lack of) you may have developed other intolerances or allergies since. I had an allergy test when I was a child, which revealed that I had an allergy to dust, which triggered my asthma. My asthma completely cleared up when I was seventeen.

But I had another allergy test when I was nineteen. It revealed that I now had an intolerance to citric acid. This explained a lot as I was constantly getting sores on my lips, gums, jaws and tongue in spite of eating fruit daily. Once I stopped having citric acid, the sores vanished.

Allergy tests don't cost much, they are painless, don't take a lot of time, and most importantly, the knowledge you receive in the test may very well save your life one day.

CHAPTER 28

YOU CAN'T PREPARE FOR EVERYTHING

The ideal situation after you get cancer is –

You have six chemotherapy sessions over three months.

Then you have twenty-five radiotherapy sessions over five weeks.

You get a check up shortly after to confirm that the cancer has either died or gone into remission.

You get a two-year check to confirm that the cancer hasn't returned. If it hasn't at this point, it is likely it will never come back.

Throughout this time, you will get medicine, injections, blood transfusions, give blood samples, have every type of scan imaginable and make many, many hospital visits.

That is ideally what should happen. I'm going to safely assume that's never happened in the history of human civilization.

A curveball will be thrown at you that you can never expect. You can't predict what it will be or when it will come.

My wife's immune system was so low after a chemo session, that a low-grade food intolerance to mushrooms became a potentially lethal allergy and she was rushed to hospital.

My father's co-ordination was so disorientated one day that he couldn't walk straight. He kept walking in circles but he thought he was walking in a straight line. We thought this was the cancer spreading to his brain. But it was a reaction from his medication. His pills were revised and his co-ordination was fine.

Not even doctors can predict what could happen to you or when or why. You need to have friends and loved ones at your beck and call at all times. Someone needs to be ready to ring the doctor or take you to hospital because during the battle for your life, you have to constantly expect the unexpected.

Although I am trying to give as many examples as possible of the universal experiences every person battling cancer will have, no two people will go through it the same way.

If you or someone close to you was recently diagnosed, you will want to talk to somebody who has had cancer.

That's a good idea. But don't settle for one person. Find out from as many cancer survivors as possible.

Even when you are at the hospital, total strangers are more than happy to talk about their cancer if they believe their experience can provide some guidance to another ill person.

My father had pancreatic cancer so I researched every famous person with the same illness to see if there were any connections. I would read their quotes and watch interviews where they talk about their experience. It can give you a lot of understanding and insight.

Because every person has a different journey, don't expect the same things to happen to different people and don't expect them to react the same way.

My mother's friend found radiotherapy easy and experienced no symptoms. But my friend, Sue, said she found radiotherapy far worse than chemo, physiotherapy or surgery.

Not only do you have to prepare for the unexpected during your treatment but after it's over. Cancer can affect your mood, your attitude, your body and your diet in the short term and the long term. Since Julie's finished her treatment, she has a few side effects. She has some nerve damage from her chemotherapy. She is more tired than she used to me. The treatment has affected her taste so she doesn't like some foods anymore.

But the most bizarre side effect was how it effected her concentration.

Julie is one of those people who is built to be in charge. She is naturally diligent, systematic, and breaks every job into lots of mini-jobs, whether it is a project at work, organizing a wedding, or cooking a Christmas turkey.

But after her treatment, her concentration waned. We thought it was because she was stressed but the doctors said that it is a common side effect.

This doesn't sound like a big deal. But this took a lot of getting used to for Julie. Julie never used to forget appointments. After her treatment, she kept getting phone calls from dentists and doctors asking why she didn't show up for her appointments. She would get so confused. It wasn't like her. It was out of character.

You know when you walk into a room and you think, "Wait...why did I walk in here again?" Julie never did that before her treatment.

Now she does it all of the time. She even bumps into stuff or trips because she zones out and isn't concentrating on her surroundings.

You know when you need an important document but you can't find it? You know when you're in a situation where you needed a proof of address or your driver's license and you were scrambling around the house desperately trying to locate it?

That never happened to Julie before she was ill. She was one of those people that filed EVERYTHING away. If she ever needed a document urgently like a birth-certificate, a work permit, details for her bank, security numbers, or a password; she had them all filed away in categorical folders (that were alphabetized and color-coded) and she could locate anything she wanted in seconds.

She believed that anyone who didn't do this was lazy.

But that mentality stopped after her treatment.

You're not expected to be strong with every factor because some things will happen that you can never prepare for. With cancer, you will be tired, you will be sore, you will be nauseous, but you will also be thrown some curveballs. And these curveballs can throw you off completely. You will need to learn to adjust yourself again.

CHAPTER 29

YOU WILL FIND JOY WHEREVER YOU CAN

When my father was in the hospice in his last few days, a nurse asked him if he was in any pain.

At this point, my father had lost seventy pounds and was so weak, he went into a coma a few days later. If a man in this dire state was asked if they were in pain, you would expect them to answer with a simple "yes" or "no." Even a grunt, a nod, or a simple hand gesture would be understandable.

But my dad did not react this way. He was a proud man who liked to impress people. So when the nurse asked him if he was in any pain, he said, ".....periodically."

My brother and I turned to each other, trying not to laugh and I said, "I have never said that word in my entire life."

At my father's wake and funeral, everyone was telling stories about him. There were many generous tales about my dad finding homes for people or visiting families who were struggling with money during Christmas or showing up at doors with free bottles of champagne.

Yeah... people didn't talk about any of those things at his funeral.

They talked about the time he pretended to be a blind beggar wandering the city or when he pretended to jump off Carrantuohill, the tallest mountain in Ireland. People had tears in their eyes but they were from joy, not grief.

The day my wife found out she had cancer, one of the first things she did was spend an hour playing with her one-year-old niece, Lilly-Mae.

When Julie needed to have a blood transfusion, she was making jokes and making her family laugh in the hospital.

Every time she had chemo, Julie and her mother and I would play scrabble (even though her mum totally cheats and adds "s" to the end of every word. You can't do that. It says so in the rulebook.)

But I digress...

In my father's last few months, he couldn't laugh without experiencing intense pain. The only times this didn't happen was hours after his chemotherapy sessions. Watching my father laugh and makes jokes again for the first time since his diagnosis is one of my fondest memories of him. It was nice to see him like his old self again, even if those moments were very brief.

Some people may find laughing and joking during times of tragedy disrespectful, but I believe those are the memories people will cherish most to their dying day.

CHAPTER 30

YOUR BODY WILL KNOW
HOW TO PROTECT YOU

One of the first things my wife said after she came out of surgery was, "I would kill to have some eggs and steak."

These foods have a huge amount of protein, which Julie was obviously lacking after she had such a massive surgical procedure.

But here's the thing; Julie didn't know steak or eggs had a huge amount of protein. Her body did.

Even if you don't intellectually know what food you should eat and what food you should avoid, your body has an astonishing ability to know exactly what you need and what you don't need.

My father had pancreatic cancer. A lot of people don't know what the pancreas does. They tend to say things like, "it has something to do with insulin or regulating your blood sugar or something like that."

Your pancreas detoxifies your bloodstream. When you eat, you absorb the nutrients and excrete everything else. However, there are certain types of bacteria in all food that should be harmful to your body but the pancreas has evolved to purify your blood to prevent bacteria from doing any harm.

But once my father's pancreas stopped working, anything he ate would kill him faster.

So you will never guess what happened next. My father's body literally turned off the section of his brain that creates hunger pangs. My dad couldn't experience hunger.

My family would give him a slice of toast or yoghurt and he would stare at it, sometimes for hours saying, "I should eat it...but I'm not hungry. I will in an hour or two."

Eight hours would pass and it would stay there by his bedside untouched. He would completely forget about it because his body was telling him that he didn't need to eat.

My dad reached a point that if he saw food, smelt food, overheard someone talk about food or even thought about food, he would feel so ill that he would sometimes vomit. This was his body's way of saying, "Don't Eat ANYTHING."

Weirdly, my father would mainly consume one thing – lemon-flavored water. I have never seen him drink this before he had cancer. But after his diagnosis, he was gulping it down everyday. I asked him if it was the doctor's recommendation. He said no. He didn't know why he was craving it so much.

I didn't think much of it until a year later when my wife was in the middle of her treatment. Julie was going to be home from work and I decided to make her pancakes. I don't know why. I never made her pancakes in my life nor do I ever eat them. My old housemate, Nigel use to make pancakes with lemon-juice so maybe there was a part of me that thought it would be good for her.

The funny thing is when Julie came home, she had bought pancakes and lemon-juice!

She never eats pancakes. Ever. I have not seen her eat a pancake once before or since. But her body was telling her to get some lemon into her.

I thought this was too much to be a coincidence and I researched it. It turns out lemon is so naturally pure that it exerts less effort to break down than almost any other food. That's why Julie and my dad were craving it. It was the only food that wouldn't take a toll on their bodies.

If you are ill and your body is screaming out for certain foods, listen to those cravings. The foods may seem obscure but your body isn't demanding these foods for fun. It's trying to protect you. It's telling you what you need.

CHAPTER 31

YOU'LL FIND OUT WHO YOUR REAL FRIENDS ARE

There are some people that you are acquainted with but you don't see them really as friends. They may be colleagues or classmates or co-workers. You might make small talk with them every now again but you don't pursue them to socialize.

But when you are in your darkest hour, you may realize that you have more friends that you ever thought. They will go the extra mile for you. Some of my friends travelled over a hundred miles to see my wife to make sure she was okay even though they had never met her until that day. Kindness like this can be the most reassuring feeling, especially when you feel like you want to give up.

I was in school at Oxford when my father was ill. I went home for a few weeks to be with him until the very end. When I returned to Oxford, some students who I have never spoken to wrote me cards to tell me they were sorry for my loss. I didn't even know some of their names.

My former housemates and classmates never contacted me after my father passed away, saying that they were "busy" or "they forgot."

When Julie was ill, the person that contacted me the most was my old classmate, Charlotte. I have been meaning to meet up with Charlotte but we've been extremely busy so I haven't seen her in over five years. When this happens with a friend, it's easy to grow distant and they eventually disappear off your radar.

When Julie was in and out of hospital, Charlotte was the lead in a play in Germany for six months so she was incredibly busy. Yet she text, rang, and Skyped me every other day. She even wrote me letters... real letters! Made of paper and everything! Nobody does that anymore! She is one of those people that never stops working but somehow always finds time for her friends.

However, not everyone will be as reliable as Charlotte was.

When I say you will find out who your real friends, I don't just mean you find out how supportive your friends are. You will also discover that some of your supposed friends aren't as deserving of your friendship as you'd imagine.

You might have friends for years, even decades who will not be there for you in your hour of need. This could happen for all sorts of reasons; fear, immaturity, lack of understanding, lack of responsibility, denial, or you simply weren't as close as you thought you were.

I heard of a horrific story on television of a pilot who had to abandon his fighter jet. The ejection malfunction so his legs were cut off as he escaped from his jet. His parachute didn't work and he plummeted thousands of feet to the ground. Miraculously he survived, even after losing a lot of blood and his legs.

But the worst thing is his wife left him days later. She couldn't take that level of responsibility.

I worked with a man two years ago called Ian who suffered brain damage after a motorcycle accident. He was in hospital for five years. As he was trying desperately to relearn how to walk again, his long-time partner left him because she didn't want to look after an invalid. This made him sink into a depression. He gave up his physiotherapy for a month. But he eventually got back on his feet (literally) and he's fine now with little side effects.

Your friends, a family member, a loved one may abandon you when you need them most and it will feel like the biggest betrayal.

But you need to focus on the people who are there for you and feed off their support to get you through your darkest hour rather than dwelling on the people who failed you. It's not your fault they are not supportive. You shouldn't go out of your way to rekindle what friendship you thought you had. Just focus on yourself and those that support you.

CHAPTER 32

YOU WILL ALWAYS BE A CANCER SURVIVOR

This may sound like a bad thing because it has the connotations of a label or stigma you can never get rid of. But it can be an incredibly positive thing.

You will always be seen as a beacon of hope.

People will pursue you when they or their loved ones become ill because they will see you as the one who has all of the answers.

When people are staring at you, it can make you upset or even angry. But people may not be staring at you out of curiosity or rudeness. It might be because they have gone through the same thing and they know how it feels.

But you won't just be connected to people. You will be connected to everything. Books, music, movies, food, heroes, stories and places can all have a greater significance.

When your friends are fighting for their lives and they feel alone, your battle with cancer will make them feel better.

My wife and I are seen by many of our friends as walking encyclopedias for cancer. Julie was asked all sorts of questions.

"Where do you get wigs?"

"Where do you get headscarves?"

"What do you do to stay sane when you are waiting six hours for the chemotherapy drugs to be pumped into your system?"

"What is the worst part?"

"How long did it take for your hair to fall out?"

"Did it fall out in clumps or completely?"

"Do you lose your eyebrows and eyelashes?"

"If you did, was that just you or does that happen to everybody?"

"Do you lose your eyebrows and eyelashes the same time as your hair?"

"What curveballs did you experience?"

"Did you genuinely consider giving up?"

"Do you think you could go through it again if you had to?"

Julie is the type of person that doesn't dwell on the past. But she is more than happy to give anyone reassuring advice about her own experience.

Sometimes, people can become very ill and they have friends who have been through similar circumstances but they don't talk to them because they don't want their friends to dredge up the past and force them to look back on a dark time in their life.

But I think its human nature that people naturally will do everything in their power to use their own experience to quell people's fears, doubts and insecurities.

You are always going to be seen as a cancer survivor. If you live for another fifty years, that is what you will be seen as. So since you can't escape it, you might as well use it for the benefit of others.

CHAPTER 33

IT'S NOT OVER EVEN AFTER IT'S OVER

Sadly, you will have to deal with the psychological side someday.

It's not uncommon for people to become depressed after they get the all-clear from their cancer. Now that they are finished with the illness physically, they finally have an opportunity to deal with it mentally. They couldn't process it when they were going through the treatment because they were just trying to get through the day and prepare for the next battle tomorrow.

If you suffer a horrible break up with a partner, you are allowed to go to pieces.

You might feel like you can't when you are fighting cancer. You might feel like you can't fall apart during chemotherapy when you know you will be starting radiotherapy in a few weeks time. As a result, a lot of the mental battle with cancer begins after the treatment ends. You can be clear from your cancer for years, even decades and you can still worry that it may come back.

My friend, Don, had skin cancer. He did the treatment for six months and he got the test results and the doctor says he had the all-clear. To ensure the cancer never returned, he had several moles on his body removed. After they were surgically removed, the doctor placed bandages on the wounds.

A day or two later, Don noticed that all of the bandages had turned green. He instantly thought it was gangrene or an infection rotting his flesh away. He panicked and called a doctor.

When the doctor saw his bandages, he explained that this is what happens when that type of bandage has contact with bacteria. The bandages are designed to change color so the doctors know when it is time to get a new one.

Unfortunately, Don's paranoia didn't end there.

A year went by. He started to get weird twinges in his stomach. He thought, "It's probably a tummy bug."

But they kept happening. He started to get paranoid and pondered to himself, "Didn't the doctor say that if the cancer returns, it will come back in the abdominal area?"

"Am I overreacting? Maybe this is one of the side effects from the radiotherapy. They said that it causes side effects. Yeah, that must be it. "

Then he started get a pins-and-needles sensation in his arm. He went straight to the doctor and they said it was nerve-damage from chemotherapy. He said, "If that's all it is, I can live with that. So long as the cancer hasn't returned."

The following week, he had a Chinese take-away. He felt funny after the food and suddenly ran to the bathroom to vomit. He looked into the toilet and saw a red substance.

Blood.

He got in contact with the hospital immediately and demanded to be checked.

The doctors scanned him and said he was perfectly healthy. Don retorted, "That's impossible! I'm not a hypochondriac! My tummy was at me, then my arm, now I'm vomiting blood! Explain that!!!"

The doctor asked him, "What was the last thing you ate?"

Then the penny dropped. Don realized what happened and embarrassingly had to admit, "Sweet and sour chicken."

The red substance in the toilet was sweet and sour sauce, not blood.

Don is not a paranoid guy. He thought his stomach pain was a tummy bug, (which it was) and he accepted that his arm pains were from his chemotherapy. It was a combination of things that made him paranoid.

If that happened to a person who didn't have cancer, they would most certainly know that the red substance was not blood.

But Don, like any cancer survivor, is constantly monitoring his health. He is looking for clues that his cancer may be returning.

It would be naive not to. But you need to find a balance. Some changes in your body will happen from age rather than an illness. You should be aware of your healthy but you shouldn't live in fear.

It's tempting to say to yourself, "Ok, I had cancer. But now I have the all-clear. It's time to close the chapter of my life." My wife finished her treatment three weeks before our wedding. Our wedding wasn't only a celebration of our love but a victory for her treatment. If her story was a movie, the wedding would have been a perfect ending.

But a "happily ever after" ending is not so simple. A few months later, my wife suffered anxiety attacks. It happened on the first day my wife was in our new house by herself and I was away at work. Since she had nobody to speak to, it gave her mind its first chance to process everything that happened to her during her treatment. Julie didn't even have a chance to process the cancer as soon as she was diagnosed. There was no warning she had cancer and as soon as she was told, she didn't get a chance to think about it because she need to have surgery eight days later.

She had just over a week to cancel bookings and holidays, make arrangements for work, tell her family and friends, prioritize her stay at the hospital and her recovery, buy everything necessary for the next few months, research about cancer, the side effects, medication, physical consequences, psychological consequences, etc.

You can't allow the cancer to control your life when the treatment is over but you need to accept that is is a part of your life.

CHAPTER 34

WE ARE GETTING BETTER AT CURING CANCER EVERY DAY

In 2012, Jack Andraka invented a biosensor for pancreatic cancer, ovarian cancer and lung cancer. His sensor is 400 times more sensitive than previous diagnostic sensors. It shows results 168 times faster than previous technology. Most importantly, the type of scans patients originally used cost at least $800 but as much as $80,000. Andraka's scan cost $3. His sensor is 26,667 times cheaper than what hospitals used only a few years ago.

The most astounding thing is that he did this when he was fifteen.

I said earlier in the book that pancreatic cancer is the most lethal cancer in the world and the fastest killing. But Andraka's research will skyrocket the survival rate of this cancer.

Brittany Wenger developed a computer algorithm that could detect breast tumors with 99% accuracy.

Shree Bose's research on a protein called AMPK has had incredible results, reducing the side effects to chemotherapy, especially fighting against ovarian cancer.

The Large Hadron Collider in Switzerland is the most complex and largest machine in the world. It is so intricate, that scientists had to advance their understanding of particle physics to operate it. This has indirectly advanced MRI scans, X-rays, CT scans, positron radioactive tomography, etc.

I could write a whole book with uplifting stories like this (I might do that next) but my point is this – In every battle, there is a winning side and a losing side and cancer is losing. There are misconceptions that cancer is on the rise. Cancer seems to be increasing because there are far more people in the world than ever before. The population of the world has septupled in the past century. So there are going to be a lot more stores about people getting cancer. You hear about cancer more often thanks to social media bombarding you with news, articles, websites, commercials, and documentaries. People can research it themselves now thanks to the Internet. Years ago, "cancer" seemed like a naughty word we couldn't mention.

The reason why people are dying from cancer more than ever is because up until a few decades ago, something else would always kill them first – cholera, tuberculosis, smallpox, poor sanitation, famine, etc. Thanks to inoculations, quarantines, and a better understanding of cleanliness, humanity is better than ever at combatting lethal threats, and that includes cancer.

We are defeating the illness with knowledge. Less than a century ago, no one knew that mosquitoes caused malaria. Malaria was considered a disease you "just got" like the flu or a cold. Malaria has been the biggest cause of human death for millennia. The death toll from malaria has plummeted over the years by the millions because we understood what it was and we figured out how to counter it.

Who knows? In the future, we might look at cancer the same way we look at smallpox or tuberculosis. In the future, it might not just be treatable but curable. We won't just use treatment to make it go into remission; we will be able to kill it. I'm not saying that a cure is going to be created one day and cancer will vanish over night. Results take time.

But it is getting better every day. A few years ago, pancreatic cancer used to be a terminal sentence that would kill patients in four weeks.

My father lived with it for seven months. It is still a lethal illness but as you can see, my father lived with it seven times longer than what was possible a decade ago. Hell, John Hurt was diagnosed with pancreatic cancer this summer and due to treatment, it has gone into remission. That NEVER happened a few years ago. Andraka's research and people like him will continue to improve cancer treatment exponentially so that one day, pancreatic cancer will have a cure. And one day, we shall have the cure for cancer itself.